THE AI ROBOT WITH THREE BRAINS

Figure 02 and All You Need To Know

*How Artificial Intelligence and Robotics
Are Ushering in a New Era of Industry and
Healthcare*

Alejandro S. Diego

Table of Contents

Introduction

In the realm of technology, few innovations have captured the imagination and potential of humanity quite like artificial intelligence and robotics. From the early days of mechanical automatons to today's sophisticated AI-driven machines, the journey of these marvels has been nothing short of extraordinary. The story of AI and robotics is a tale of relentless innovation, ambition, and the pursuit of a future where the lines between human capabilities and machine potential blur.

As we stand on the brink of a new era, two groundbreaking developments have emerged, promising to redefine industries and transform our everyday lives. Enter the Figure 02 robot, a testament to the strides made in humanoid robotics. Sleek, powerful, and intelligent, this robot represents a significant leap forward from its predecessor, Figure 01. Gone are the bulky, exposed wires and chrome-plated exterior. In their place, we find a streamlined, matte black marvel engineered for real-world applications. With its refined design, enhanced battery life, and unparalleled dexterity, Figure 02 is not just a robot; it is a vision of the future in motion.

Imagine a robot with hands almost as flexible as yours, capable of lifting heavy objects with ease, navigating complex environments with precision, and understanding voice commands as naturally as a human. Picture this machine working alongside humans on a production line, its movements fluid and purposeful, its tasks executed with impeccable accuracy. This is not a distant dream but a present reality, made possible by cutting-edge advancements in AI and robotics.

Yet, the wonders of modern technology do not stop there. Imagine a scenario where dental surgery, a procedure that traditionally requires multiple visits and considerable time, is performed autonomously by a robot. This is the promise of the AI robot dentist developed by Perceptive. Utilizing advanced AI algorithms, 3D imaging, and robotics, this machine can diagnose and treat dental issues with an accuracy rate surpassing 90%. In a fraction of the time it would take a human dentist, this robot can place crowns, all without the need for invasive radiation.

These innovations are more than just technical marvels; they signify a profound shift in how we interact with technology. The Figure 02 robot and the AI robot dentist embody the potential of AI and robotics to enhance efficiency, reduce human error, and open new frontiers in both industrial and healthcare applications. They represent a world where robots are not confined to the pages of science fiction but are active participants in our daily lives, performing tasks once thought to be the exclusive domain of humans.

The significance of these developments cannot be overstated. As industries and healthcare systems grapple with the challenges of efficiency, accuracy, and cost, the introduction of advanced AI robots offers a glimpse into a future where these obstacles are overcome with unprecedented elegance and precision. The Figure 02 robot, with its advanced capabilities and real-world applications, and the AI robot dentist, with its promise of revolutionizing dental care, are harbingers of this new era.

As you turn the pages of this book, prepare to embark on a journey through the fascinating world of AI and robotics. Discover the intricate details of these technological wonders, understand their impact on various sectors, and envision the future they are poised to create. The story of AI and robotics is one of innovation, transformation, and limitless possibilities. Welcome to the future. Welcome to a world where machines not only think but also transform our reality in ways we are only beginning to understand.

Chapter 1: The Evolution of Humanoid Robots

The journey of humanoid robots has been marked by relentless innovation and visionary ambition. From the initial rudimentary mechanical constructs to the sophisticated machines we see today, each step in this evolution has brought us closer to realizing the dream of creating robots that can seamlessly integrate into human environments.

In the early days, the concept of humanoid robots was largely confined to the realms of science fiction and speculative engineering. The first attempts were clunky, mechanical creations that could perform basic tasks but were far from being practical or versatile. These early robots were limited by the technology of their time, relying on simple motors and basic programming to perform a narrow range of actions. Despite their limitations, these initial developments laid the groundwork for the future, sparking the imagination of engineers and scientists who envisioned a world where robots could think, move, and act with the fluidity of a human.

As technology advanced, so too did the capabilities of humanoid robots. The introduction of more sophisticated sensors, improved materials, and advanced computing power led to the creation of robots that could perform more complex tasks with greater precision. One of the most notable milestones in this journey was the development of Figure 01, a robot that represented a significant leap forward in both design and functionality. Figure 01 was designed to withstand rigorous testing in laboratory environments, featuring a robust, chrome-plated exterior that was as functional as it was imposing. This robot was a testament to the possibilities of humanoid robotics, showcasing the potential for machines to perform tasks that were previously thought to be the exclusive domain of humans.

However, while Figure 01 was a remarkable achievement, it was not without its shortcomings.

The bulky design and exposed wiring, while suitable for a controlled environment, posed challenges for real-world applications. It was clear that for humanoid robots to move beyond the lab and into everyday use, further refinement was needed.

This realization led to the development of Figure 02, a robot that represents the next generation of humanoid machines. With Figure 02, engineers took everything they learned from the first model and pushed the boundaries even further. One of the most striking differences between Figure 01 and Figure 02 is the design. Gone is the bulky, chrome-plated exterior; in its place is a sleek, matte black finish that exudes modernity and sophistication. This new design is not just about aesthetics; it reflects a deeper understanding of the functional needs of a humanoid robot in a real-world setting.

The transition from Figure 01 to Figure 02 was marked by several key improvements. One of the most significant changes was the integration of the robot's cabling. In Figure 01, the wires were intentionally exposed to allow for easy adjustments and repairs during testing. However, in Figure 02, the cabling is neatly tucked away inside the robot's limbs, protecting it from environmental damage and giving the robot a cleaner, more streamlined appearance. This change not only enhances the robot's durability but also improves its safety and reliability in industrial applications.

Another major enhancement in Figure 02 is the battery design. The new model features a battery that provides over 50% more energy than its predecessor, integrated into the robot's torso to optimize balance and agility. This improvement allows Figure 02 to work longer hours and perform more demanding tasks with greater efficiency. The enhanced battery life, combined with the robot's refined design, makes Figure 02 a more practical and versatile tool for a wide range of applications.

The hands of Figure 02 are another area where significant advancements have been made. With 16 degrees of freedom, the hands can move with a level of dexterity that closely mimics human movement. This increased flexibility allows the robot to manipulate objects with greater precision and strength, lifting up to 25 kilograms, a substantial improvement over Figure 01's 20-kilogram capacity. These enhancements make Figure 02 not just a tool but a partner in industrial environments, capable of performing tasks that require both strength and finesse.

The evolution from Figure 01 to Figure 02 is a testament to the rapid advancements in humanoid robotics. Each iteration builds on the successes and lessons of its predecessors, pushing the boundaries of what is possible. As we continue to refine and improve these machines, we move closer to a future where humanoid robots are not just a novelty but an integral part of our daily lives. The journey of humanoid robots is far from over, and with each new development, we are reminded of the limitless potential of human ingenuity and technological innovation.

Chapter 2: Technological Advancements in Figure 02

The Figure 02 robot stands as a beacon of technological prowess, embodying a series of significant advancements that elevate it far beyond its predecessors. These improvements are not merely incremental; they represent a fundamental rethinking of how a humanoid robot should be engineered and function. Central to these advancements are the internal engineering refinements, enhanced hand dexterity, and increased strength and load capacity.

One of the most profound changes in Figure 02 is the internal engineering. In the past, humanoid robots like Figure 01 had their wiring systems exposed. This design choice was intentional, allowing for quick and easy adjustments during the rigorous testing phases. However, such a setup was far from ideal for real-world applications where environmental factors could damage the exposed cables. Figure 02 addresses this issue with a meticulously refined cabling system. The wires are now ingeniously integrated within the robot's limbs, shielded from external hazards. This not only enhances the robot's durability but also contributes to a more streamlined and visually appealing design. The internal cabling is a critical step toward making humanoid robots viable for extended use in diverse industrial settings, where reliability and robustness are paramount.

Equally impressive is the battery integration in Figure 02. Previous models often struggled with limited operational time, a significant drawback for continuous industrial applications. Figure 02 overcomes this limitation with a battery that offers over 50% more energy than its predecessor. This battery is cleverly embedded within the robot's torso, optimizing the center of mass for better balance and agility. This placement ensures that the robot remains stable while performing a variety of tasks, reducing the risk of toppling over and enhancing overall efficiency. The enhanced battery life allows Figure 02 to work longer shifts without needing frequent recharges, making it a more practical and reliable solution for industries looking to automate their processes.

The advancements in Figure 02's hand dexterity are another cornerstone of its technological leap. The robot's hands are designed with 16 degrees of freedom, allowing them to move with a level of finesse and flexibility that closely mirrors the human hand. This degree of freedom is crucial for performing tasks that require intricate movements and precise control. Whether it's assembling small components, handling delicate objects, or performing complex manipulations, Figure 02's hands can execute these tasks with remarkable accuracy. This enhanced dexterity opens up a myriad of possibilities for the robot's application, from manufacturing and assembly lines to service industries where delicate handling is essential.

Beyond dexterity, the strength and load capacity of Figure 02 have seen substantial improvements. The robot can now lift and carry up to 25 kilograms, a significant increase from the 20-kilogram capacity of Figure 01. This enhancement not only boosts the robot's utility in heavy-duty applications but also showcases its ability to handle a wider range of tasks. The combination of strength and precision makes Figure 02 a versatile tool in environments that demand both robustness and delicacy. The robot's ability to carry heavier loads without compromising on movement efficiency or stability is a testament to the advanced engineering that underpins its design.

The technological advancements embodied in Figure 02 are a testament to the relentless pursuit of innovation in the field of robotics. Each improvement, from the refined internal cabling and enhanced battery integration to the sophisticated hand dexterity and increased load capacity, represents a significant step forward in making humanoid robots a practical and valuable asset in industrial and commercial applications. These advancements not only enhance the robot's performance but also broaden the scope of what is possible with robotic technology. Figure 02 is not just a machine; it is a glimpse into the future of automation, where robots can seamlessly integrate into human environments, performing tasks with a level of efficiency and precision that was once the stuff of science fiction. As we continue to push the boundaries of what robots can do, the potential for transformative change in how we live and work becomes ever more tangible.

Chapter 3: Autonomy and Intelligence

The Figure 02 robot epitomizes the cutting edge of artificial intelligence and robotics, particularly in its vision and perception, voice interaction, and computational power. These advancements not only distinguish it from its predecessors but also place it at the forefront of humanoid robot development.

Vision and perception are fundamental to the Figure 02 robot's ability to navigate and interact with its environment. Equipped with six onboard cameras, the robot can achieve a comprehensive 360-degree view of its surroundings. These cameras are strategically positioned to provide overlapping fields of vision, ensuring no blind spots and enabling the robot to perceive depth and movement accurately. This visual capability is further enhanced by a sophisticated vision language model, which processes the raw data from the cameras and translates it into meaningful information. This model allows the robot to identify objects, understand spatial relationships, and interpret complex scenes. Whether it is picking up objects, avoiding obstacles, or navigating through dynamic environments, Figure 02 can perform these tasks autonomously and with remarkable precision.

The vision system's integration with advanced AI enables Figure 02 to understand and react to its environment much like a human. For instance, if an unexpected obstacle appears in its path, the robot can quickly assess the situation and choose an appropriate course of action, such as stopping, altering its path, or picking up the object. This level of autonomy is a significant leap forward in the field of robotics, demonstrating the potential for robots to function independently in complex, real-world scenarios.

Voice interaction is another area where Figure 02 excels, making human-robot communication more intuitive and natural. Unlike previous models that required pre-programmed commands, Figure 02 can understand and respond to a wide range of spoken instructions. This capability is powered by onboard microphones and speakers, coupled with custom AI models developed in partnership with OpenAI. These models enable the robot to process natural language, understand context, and engage in conversations. Users can ask Figure 02 to perform specific tasks, inquire about its status, or seek information about its surroundings, and the robot can respond accurately and promptly.

The voice interaction system is designed to handle not only simple commands but also more complex conversational exchanges. For example, if asked about the objects on a table, Figure 02 can describe their positions and potentially their uses. This interactive capability is akin to conversing with a knowledgeable assistant, making the robot a valuable asset in various settings, from industrial floors to service environments. The ease of communication through voice commands significantly enhances the robot's usability, making it accessible to users with little to no technical background.

At the heart of Figure 02's advanced capabilities lies its enhanced computational power. The robot is equipped with three times the computational power and AI inference capabilities compared to Figure 01. This increase in processing power allows Figure 02 to analyze vast amounts of data in real-time, making decisions and executing tasks with unprecedented speed and efficiency. The enhanced AI inference capabilities mean that the robot can better understand and interpret the data from its sensors, leading to more accurate and reliable performance.

Real-time processing is crucial for the robot's autonomy and effectiveness. Whether it's recognizing a sudden change in its environment, processing complex tasks, or interacting with humans, Figure 02 can do so swiftly and efficiently. This real-time capability is essential for applications that require immediate responses, such as emergency situations, high-speed manufacturing processes, or dynamic service environments.

The combination of advanced vision and perception, sophisticated voice interaction, and powerful computational abilities makes Figure 02 a versatile and highly capable humanoid robot. These technological advancements not only enhance the robot's functionality but also broaden the range of applications where it can be effectively utilized. Figure 02 represents a significant milestone in the evolution of robotics, showcasing how far we have come and offering a glimpse into the future possibilities of AI and robotic integration into everyday life. As we continue to innovate and refine these technologies, the potential for humanoid robots to transform industries and improve human life becomes increasingly within reach.

Chapter 4: Real-World Applications

The deployment of Figure 02 in industrial settings marks a significant milestone in the evolution of humanoid robots. The partnership with BMW is a testament to the robot's advanced capabilities and its potential to revolutionize manufacturing processes. This collaboration was initiated to test the robot's performance in a real-world industrial environment, moving beyond controlled laboratory conditions to face the complexities and demands of a functioning production line.

In the BMW plant in South Carolina, Figure 02 has been put to work alongside human employees, handling tasks that range from the mundane to the intricate. The results of these tests have been promising. Figure 02's ability to perform repetitive tasks with consistent precision has significantly reduced the margin of error, a common issue in human labor due to fatigue and inconsistency. The robot's advanced vision system allows it to navigate the factory floor seamlessly, avoiding obstacles and dynamically adjusting to changes in its environment. This adaptability is crucial in a busy industrial setting where unforeseen circumstances can arise at any moment.

One of the standout features of Figure 02 in these industrial tests has been its dexterity and strength. The robot's hands, with their 16 degrees of freedom, have demonstrated the ability to handle delicate components and heavy parts with equal ease. This dual capability is a game-changer for assembly lines, where tasks can vary widely in their requirements for precision and force. Moreover, the robot's increased load capacity means it can carry heavier items than its predecessors, further expanding the range of tasks it can perform.

The integration of Figure 02 into BMW's production line has also highlighted the benefits of its enhanced computational power. The robot can process information in real-time, allowing it to make quick decisions and adjustments. This capability has proven invaluable in optimizing workflow and increasing overall efficiency. For example, Figure 02 can detect when a part is out of place and either correct it autonomously or alert human supervisors, thereby preventing potential disruptions and ensuring a smooth production process.

The implications of these real-world tests extend far beyond the BMW plant. The success of Figure 02 in this setting suggests a broad potential for the robot's deployment across various industries. Manufacturing, logistics, healthcare, and even service industries can benefit from the capabilities of advanced humanoid robots. In manufacturing, robots like Figure 02 can take on repetitive and physically demanding tasks, reducing the risk of injury to human workers and improving productivity. In logistics, their ability to handle packages with care and efficiency can streamline operations and enhance accuracy. In healthcare, robots can assist with tasks ranging from patient care to surgical procedures, bringing precision and consistency to critical functions.

The future prospects for the widespread adoption of humanoid robots are vast. As technology continues to advance, we can expect these robots to become more capable and affordable, making them accessible to a wider range of businesses. The integration of AI and robotics will likely lead to the development of even more sophisticated machines, capable of performing a broader spectrum of tasks with greater autonomy and intelligence.

Moreover, the societal impact of such advancements cannot be understated. The deployment of humanoid robots in various sectors could lead to significant changes in the job market, with robots taking over tasks that are dangerous, repetitive, or require high precision. This shift could free up human workers to engage in more creative and strategic roles, fostering innovation and growth in new areas. However, it also raises important questions about workforce adaptation and the need for new skills training programs to prepare individuals for the evolving job landscape.

In conclusion, the industrial deployment of Figure 02 through its partnership with BMW showcases the immense potential of advanced humanoid robots. The positive results from real-world testing underscore the viability of these machines in enhancing efficiency, precision, and safety in various settings. As we look to the future, the widespread adoption of humanoid robots promises to usher in a new era of technological integration, transforming industries and redefining the way we work and live. The journey of Figure 02 is just the beginning, and the possibilities for the future are boundless.

Chapter 5: Breakthrough in Medical Robotics

In the ever-evolving landscape of artificial intelligence and robotics, one of the most remarkable advancements has emerged in the field of healthcare: the AI robot dentist developed by Perceptive. This groundbreaking innovation represents a significant leap forward in autonomous medical procedures, offering a glimpse into a future where robots can perform complex tasks with minimal human intervention. Perceptive's AI robot dentist is not only a marvel of engineering but also a harbinger of a new era in dental care, where efficiency, precision, and accessibility are redefined.

The introduction of Perceptive's autonomous dental robot has captured the attention of both the medical and technological communities. Unlike traditional dental practices that rely heavily on human expertise and manual dexterity, this robot leverages advanced AI algorithms, 3D imaging, and robotics to perform dental procedures with a level of accuracy and speed that surpasses human capabilities. The robot's ability to operate autonomously marks a significant departure from the conventional methods of dental care, promising to revolutionize the industry.

One of the most compelling aspects of Perceptive's AI robot dentist is its procedure capabilities. Traditionally, procedures such as placing crowns involve multiple visits to the dentist, with each visit requiring significant time and effort. The AI robot dentist streamlines this process by performing the entire procedure in a single session that lasts only about 15 minutes. This efficiency is made possible by the robot's ability to diagnose, plan, and execute the procedure autonomously.

The robot begins the process with a detailed diagnostic phase using a technology called 3D volumetric data imaging. This involves capturing highly detailed 3D images of the patient's teeth and gums, providing a comprehensive view that goes beyond what traditional X-rays can offer. The use of Optical Coherence Technology (OCT) further enhances this imaging process. OCT is a non-invasive imaging technique that captures detailed cross-sectional images of the dental structures. Unlike traditional imaging methods, OCT can penetrate beneath the gum line and through fluids, providing a clear and detailed view of the underlying dental structures without exposing the patient to ionizing radiation.

Once the diagnostic images are obtained, the AI algorithms analyze the data to develop a precise treatment plan. This plan includes the exact placement and fit of the crown, taking into account the unique contours and characteristics of the patient's teeth. The robot then proceeds with the treatment phase, utilizing its advanced robotic arms and tools to perform the procedure with meticulous precision. The entire process is monitored in real-time, with the AI making continuous adjustments to ensure optimal outcomes.

The technological process underlying these capabilities is a fusion of advanced imaging, AI-driven analysis, and robotic precision. The 3D volumetric data provides the foundational information needed for accurate diagnosis and planning, while the Optical Coherence Technology ensures that the imaging is detailed and non-invasive. The AI algorithms process this data, translating it into actionable insights that guide the robotic arms during the procedure. This integration of technologies allows the robot to perform tasks with a level of accuracy and efficiency that significantly reduces the margin for error.

The implications of Perceptive's AI robot dentist extend far beyond the realm of dental care. By demonstrating the feasibility of fully autonomous medical procedures, this innovation paves the way for similar advancements in other areas of healthcare. The potential benefits are immense: reduced waiting times, increased access to high-quality care, and the elimination of human error in routine procedures. Moreover, the efficiency of the AI robot dentist could lead to cost reductions, making dental care more affordable and accessible to a broader population.

As we consider the broader impact of this technology, it is clear that the AI robot dentist represents a transformative shift in how we approach medical care. The ability to diagnose and treat patients with such precision and speed opens up new possibilities for healthcare delivery. It also raises important questions about the future role of human practitioners and the need for new training and adaptation strategies in the medical field.

In conclusion, the AI robot dentist developed by Perceptive is a testament to the incredible potential of combining artificial intelligence, advanced imaging, and robotics. This innovation not only enhances the efficiency and accuracy of dental procedures but also offers a glimpse into a future where autonomous medical robots play a crucial role in healthcare. As we continue to explore and refine these technologies, the promise of a new era in medical care becomes ever more tangible, driven by the relentless pursuit of excellence and innovation.

Chapter 6: Impact on Healthcare

The introduction of Perceptive's AI robot dentist marks a transformative moment in dental care, bringing unprecedented efficiency and accuracy to procedures that have traditionally relied on human expertise. The benefits of this robotic innovation extend beyond mere technical prowess, profoundly enhancing the patient experience and setting the stage for future advancements. However, the path to widespread adoption is not without its challenges, particularly in terms of regulatory approvals and public acceptance.

One of the most significant benefits of robotic dental procedures is the dramatic increase in efficiency and accuracy. Traditional dental procedures, such as placing crowns, typically require multiple visits, each involving significant time and coordination. The AI robot dentist revolutionizes this process by completing the entire procedure in a single session. The robot's ability to diagnose, plan, and execute the treatment autonomously ensures that each step is performed with precision, minimizing the risk of errors. This high level of accuracy is achieved through the integration of advanced 3D imaging and AI-driven analysis, which provide detailed insights into the patient's dental structure and inform the robot's actions.

The efficiency of robotic dental procedures translates into tangible benefits for both patients and practitioners. For patients, the reduction in the number of visits means less time spent in the dentist's chair and fewer disruptions to their daily lives. The streamlined process also reduces the overall treatment time, allowing more patients to receive care within the same timeframe. For dental practitioners, the robot's ability to handle routine procedures with consistent precision frees up their time to focus on more complex cases and patient care, potentially increasing the practice's capacity and productivity.

Another crucial advantage of robotic dental procedures is the enhancement of the patient experience. Traditional dental treatments often involve discomfort and anxiety, particularly due to the invasive nature of some procedures. The AI robot dentist addresses these concerns by employing non-invasive technologies such as Optical Coherence Technology (OCT), which captures detailed images without the need for harmful radiation. This non-invasive approach not only improves the safety of the procedures but also reduces the discomfort associated with traditional imaging techniques.

The reduction in procedure time is another significant advantage for patients. The ability to complete treatments in a fraction of the time traditionally required means that patients spend less time undergoing potentially stressful procedures. This swift and efficient process is especially beneficial for those who experience dental anxiety, as it minimizes their exposure to the clinical environment. Additionally, the precision and accuracy of the robot ensure that the outcomes are consistently high-quality, reducing the likelihood of complications or the need for follow-up treatments.

Despite the clear benefits, the widespread adoption of robotic dental procedures faces several challenges, particularly in terms of regulatory approvals and public acceptance. Regulatory bodies, such as the US Food and Drug Administration (FDA), play a crucial role in ensuring the safety and efficacy of new medical technologies. For Perceptive's AI robot dentist to be widely deployed, it must undergo rigorous testing and validation to meet these regulatory standards. This process can be lengthy and complex, requiring comprehensive clinical trials and peer-reviewed studies to demonstrate the robot's safety and effectiveness.

Public acceptance is another critical factor in the successful integration of robotic dental procedures.

While the benefits are clear to those within the medical and technological fields, convincing the general public to trust and embrace this new technology can be challenging. Dental care is deeply personal, and many patients may have reservations about allowing a robot to perform procedures traditionally done by a human dentist. Addressing these concerns requires transparent communication about the robot's capabilities, safety measures, and the rigorous testing it undergoes. Educating patients about the advantages and demonstrating successful outcomes through pilot programs and testimonials can help build trust and acceptance.

In conclusion, the AI robot dentist developed by Perceptive represents a significant advancement in dental care, offering enhanced efficiency, accuracy, and patient experience. The benefits of reduced procedure times and non-invasive techniques are clear, providing a compelling case for the integration of robotic technology in dental practices. However, the journey to widespread adoption will require overcoming regulatory hurdles and gaining public trust. As these challenges are addressed, the potential for robotic dental procedures to transform the industry becomes increasingly apparent, heralding a new era of precision and innovation in healthcare.

Chapter 7: The Financial and Economic Implications

The development and deployment of advanced AI robots, such as Figure 02 and the AI robot dentist, have been fueled by significant financial backing and strategic investments. Companies like Figure AI and Perceptive have attracted substantial funding from investors who recognize the transformative potential of these technologies. The economic implications of these innovations are profound, promising to revolutionize various sectors and offering considerable cost-benefit advantages.

The journey of Figure AI and Perceptive from conceptualization to deployment has been supported by impressive financial investments. Figure AI, for instance, has raised a staggering $675 million in funding. This substantial capital infusion has enabled the company to push the boundaries of humanoid robotics, refining their designs, and expanding their capabilities. The partnership with

BMW, a major automotive manufacturer, underscores the strategic importance of these investments. Such collaborations not only provide financial resources but also offer real-world testing environments to validate and enhance the robots' functionalities.

Similarly, Perceptive has garnered significant support for its pioneering work in autonomous dental robotics. With $30 million in funding, the company has been able to develop and refine its AI robot dentist, integrating advanced technologies like 3D volumetric data imaging and Optical Coherence Technology. High-profile backers, including Mark Zuckerberg's father, Dr. Edward Zuckerberg, who is a dentist himself, have lent credibility and visibility to the project. These investments are a testament to the confidence that stakeholders have in the potential of AI and robotics to revolutionize healthcare.

The economic impact of these innovations extends across multiple sectors. In manufacturing, the deployment of humanoid robots like Figure 02 can lead to significant improvements in efficiency and productivity. By automating repetitive and labor-intensive tasks, these robots reduce the risk of human error and workplace injuries, leading to cost savings and enhanced output quality. In logistics, robots can streamline operations, from sorting and packaging to transportation, thus increasing accuracy and reducing delivery times.

In the healthcare sector, the introduction of autonomous robots promises to alleviate some of the critical challenges faced by the industry. For example, the AI robot dentist can perform procedures more quickly and accurately than traditional methods, reducing the burden on dental practitioners and increasing patient throughput. This efficiency can lead to lower operational costs and improved access to high-quality care, especially in underserved areas.

The cost-benefit analysis of deploying AI robots in industries and healthcare reveals compelling economic advantages. In industries, the initial investment in robotic technology can be offset by the long-term savings in labor costs and productivity gains. Robots like Figure 02 can work longer hours without fatigue, perform tasks with consistent precision, and reduce the need for costly rework. These efficiencies translate into substantial cost savings and a quicker return on investment.

In healthcare, the economic benefits are equally significant. The AI robot dentist, for instance, can perform procedures in a fraction of the time required by human dentists, leading to increased patient turnover and reduced waiting times. This efficiency can lower the overall cost of dental care, making it more affordable and accessible. Additionally, the precision of robotic procedures minimizes the risk of complications and follow-up treatments, further reducing healthcare costs.

The broader economic impact also includes the potential for job creation in new fields. As industries and healthcare systems adopt these advanced technologies, there will be a growing demand for professionals skilled in AI, robotics, and data analysis. This shift can spur innovation and create new employment opportunities, driving economic growth.

However, the transition to a more automated workforce also raises important considerations regarding workforce adaptation and retraining. As robots take over routine and labor-intensive tasks, it will be crucial to provide training programs to help workers transition to new roles that leverage human creativity, problem-solving, and interpersonal skills. Addressing these challenges proactively can ensure that the economic benefits of AI and robotics are widely shared and contribute to sustainable growth.

In conclusion, the financial backing and investments in companies like Figure AI and Perceptive highlight the significant potential of AI and robotics to transform various sectors. The economic impact of these innovations is profound, offering substantial cost-benefit advantages and promising to revolutionize industries and healthcare. As we navigate the transition to a more automated future, it will be essential to balance technological advancements with workforce adaptation to maximize the economic and societal benefits of these groundbreaking technologies.

Chapter 8: Ethical and Social Considerations

The rise of autonomous robots, such as Figure 02 and Perceptive's AI robot dentist, brings with it a host of ethical questions and societal considerations. As these advanced machines integrate more deeply into various sectors, it's crucial to explore the moral implications, potential effects on the job market, and public perception. Understanding and addressing these issues will be key to ensuring that the benefits of AI and robotics are realized in a way that is ethical and socially responsible.

One of the foremost ethical questions surrounding autonomous robots is the moral implications of their use in roles traditionally occupied by humans. As robots take on more responsibilities, particularly in areas like healthcare and manufacturing, the question of accountability arises. Who is responsible if a robot makes a mistake that results in harm? This issue is especially pertinent in medical contexts, where the stakes are incredibly high. The development of clear regulatory frameworks and accountability measures will be essential to address these ethical concerns. Additionally, there is the question of consent and autonomy. In healthcare, for example, patients must be fully informed and give consent to procedures performed by robots, understanding both the potential benefits and risks involved.

Another critical consideration is the potential impact on the job market. The introduction of autonomous robots capable of performing complex tasks could lead to significant job displacement in certain sectors. While robots can enhance efficiency and reduce costs, they may also replace human workers in roles that involve repetitive or physically demanding tasks. This shift could lead to economic and social challenges, particularly for those whose skills are closely aligned with tasks that can be automated. To mitigate these impacts, it is vital to invest in retraining and education programs that equip workers with the skills needed for new roles in an increasingly automated world. Fostering a workforce that can adapt to technological changes will be crucial in ensuring that the benefits of robotics are shared broadly and do not exacerbate existing inequalities.

The public perception of AI robots is another factor that will influence their widespread adoption. Trust and acceptance are crucial for integrating robots into daily life, particularly in sensitive areas like healthcare. Public concerns often center around the reliability and safety of autonomous robots, as well as the broader implications of their use. Transparent communication about the capabilities and limitations of these technologies is essential to build trust. Demonstrating the successful implementation of robots in real-world scenarios, along with robust safety and ethical standards, can help alleviate public apprehensions.

Moreover, the portrayal of robots in media and popular culture can significantly influence public perception. While many people are fascinated by the potential of AI and robotics, there is also a degree of fear and skepticism fueled by dystopian narratives. Educating the public about the realistic benefits and limitations of robots, rather than sensationalizing their capabilities, can help foster a more balanced understanding. Highlighting the ways in which robots can complement human efforts and improve quality of life will be key to gaining public acceptance.

In conclusion, the ethical questions, job market impacts, and public perception of autonomous robots are complex issues that require careful consideration and proactive management. Addressing the moral implications of robotic accountability and consent, investing in workforce retraining and education, and fostering trust through transparency and public engagement are critical steps in ensuring that the integration of AI and robotics into society is both beneficial and responsible. As we navigate this technological transformation, a balanced approach that considers ethical, economic, and social dimensions will be essential to harness the full potential of these groundbreaking innovations while minimizing adverse effects.

Chapter 9: The Future of AI and Robotics

As the development and deployment of advanced AI robots continue to progress, ongoing research and future directions promise to further enhance their capabilities and applications. The current trends in AI and robotics are focused on improving autonomy, interaction, and integration into diverse environments. These efforts are complemented by expert predictions and speculations on the future landscape, which envision a world where robots play an integral role in both industry and daily life. To fully realize the benefits of these advancements, it is essential for industries and individuals to prepare and adapt to the changes ahead.

Ongoing research in AI and robotics is driving several key trends. One of the most prominent areas of focus is enhancing the autonomy of robots. Researchers are working on developing more sophisticated algorithms that enable robots to perform increasingly complex tasks without human intervention. This includes advancements in machine learning, computer vision, and natural language processing. The goal is to create robots that can understand and respond to their environment with greater precision and flexibility, making them more useful in a wider range of applications.

Another significant trend is the improvement of human-robot interaction. Efforts are being made to make robots more intuitive and user-friendly, allowing for seamless communication and collaboration with humans. This includes refining voice recognition and response systems, as well as developing more expressive and adaptable physical interfaces. Enhancing the ability of robots to understand and interpret human emotions and behaviors is also a key research area, aimed at creating more empathetic and effective robotic assistants.

Integration into diverse environments is another major focus of ongoing research. Robots are being designed to operate not only in controlled industrial settings but also in more unpredictable and dynamic environments such as homes, hospitals, and public spaces. This involves improving the robustness and adaptability of robots to handle a variety of tasks and conditions. For example, advances in mobility and manipulation capabilities are enabling robots to navigate complex terrains and perform delicate operations with high precision.

Experts in the field of AI and robotics offer a range of predictions and speculations about the future landscape. Many believe that we are on the cusp of a new era where robots will become ubiquitous in both professional and personal contexts. In industries, robots are expected to take on an ever-greater share of tasks, from manufacturing and logistics to service and maintenance. This shift will likely lead to significant increases in productivity and efficiency, as well as the creation of new business models and opportunities.

In healthcare, the role of robots is predicted to expand significantly. Autonomous medical robots, such as Perceptive's AI robot dentist, are expected to become more common, performing a variety of procedures with high precision and efficiency. These advancements could lead to improved patient outcomes, reduced costs, and increased access to care, particularly in underserved areas. Additionally, robots could play a crucial role in elder care, providing assistance and companionship to aging populations.

In daily life, robots are anticipated to become more integrated into households, assisting with chores, providing security, and even offering companionship. The development of social robots that can engage in meaningful interactions with humans is expected to transform how we live and interact with technology. These robots could help alleviate loneliness, provide educational support, and enhance overall quality of life.

To prepare for these advancements, industries and individuals need to take proactive steps. For industries, this means investing in research and development to stay at the forefront of technological innovation. It also involves rethinking business processes and strategies to incorporate robotic capabilities effectively. Training programs and reskilling initiatives will be essential to ensure that the workforce can adapt to new roles and collaborate effectively with robots. Companies will need to foster a culture of continuous learning and adaptability to thrive in an increasingly automated world.

For individuals, preparing for the future of AI and robotics involves staying informed about technological trends and acquiring new skills. Lifelong learning will be crucial as the pace of technological change accelerates. Embracing flexibility and adaptability will help individuals navigate the evolving job landscape and seize new opportunities. Understanding how to work alongside robots and leveraging their capabilities to enhance productivity and creativity will be key skills in the future workplace.

In conclusion, the ongoing research in AI and robotics is driving significant advancements that promise to transform industries and daily life. Experts predict a future where robots are ubiquitous, enhancing productivity, efficiency, and quality of life. To fully realize these benefits, it is essential for industries and individuals to prepare and adapt to these changes. By embracing innovation, investing in education and training, and fostering a culture of adaptability, we can navigate the technological transformation and harness the full potential of AI and robotics for a brighter future.

Conclusion

The journey through the world of advanced AI and robotics reveals a landscape rich with innovation and potential. From the early developments of humanoid robots to the sophisticated capabilities of Figure 02 and the groundbreaking achievements of Perceptive's AI robot dentist, we have explored significant milestones that are shaping the future of technology and its applications in various sectors.

The advancements in AI and robotics are characterized by remarkable strides in autonomy, interaction, and integration. Figure 02 exemplifies these advancements with its refined internal engineering, enhanced hand dexterity, and increased strength and load capacity. Its deployment in industrial settings, particularly in partnership with BMW, demonstrates its practical utility and the positive impact on efficiency and productivity. Similarly, Perceptive's AI robot dentist showcases the transformative potential of autonomous medical robots, offering precision, efficiency, and enhanced patient experiences through advanced imaging and AI-driven procedures.

These innovations are not merely technical achievements; they signify a profound shift in how we approach manufacturing, healthcare, and everyday tasks. The economic implications are substantial, promising cost savings, improved productivity, and new opportunities across various industries. However, the ethical considerations, potential job market impacts, and public perception challenges highlight the need for thoughtful integration and proactive management.

Looking ahead, ongoing research continues to push the boundaries of what AI and robotics can achieve. The trends in enhancing robot autonomy, improving human-robot interaction, and integrating robots into diverse environments indicate a future where these machines become ubiquitous. Experts predict that robots will play an increasingly integral role in both professional and personal contexts, transforming industries and enhancing the quality of life.

The broader implications of these advancements extend beyond technological innovation. They challenge us to reconsider our relationship with machines and the future of work. The integration of robots into daily life and various sectors requires a collaborative approach, where industries and individuals adapt and prepare for the changes ahead. Investing in education, reskilling, and fostering a culture of continuous learning will be crucial to navigate this transition successfully.

As we conclude this exploration, it is essential to recognize that the story of AI and robotics is still unfolding. The rapid pace of technological change demands that we stay informed and engaged with developments. By embracing innovation and remaining proactive, we can ensure that the benefits of these advancements are realized while addressing the ethical and societal challenges they present.

In closing, I encourage you, the reader, to continue your journey into the world of AI and robotics. Stay curious, stay informed, and actively engage with the technological advancements shaping our future. Whether you are a professional in the field, a student, or simply a curious mind, your understanding and participation are vital in navigating the exciting and transformative path ahead. Together, we can harness the full potential of AI and robotics to create a future that is innovative, inclusive, and beneficial for all.